© Copyright 2021 by Ken Knorr

All rights reserved

NExTExT, LLC
Richmond, VA

ISBN 9798713415020

Collected & arranged by Tony Gentry
Cover Design by Stephen Gentry
Cover Art "Heron" by Carol Baron

Grateful acknowledgment to *Ashé Journal, Cancer Poetry Project, Crone, Earth's Daughters, Moondance, Sage Women, Sisters Singing, Tough Times Companion,* and *Women Artist's Datebook,* in which several of these poems first appeared.

Collected Poems

Sarah Knorr

NEXTEXT books

2021

Contents

Spring Planting   1
Jive Child   2
Infusion   3
Where it Comes From/Deep Within   5
Litmus Test   6
Accommodation   7
L'arc-en-ciel   8
That Time of Year   9
Still Life with Buttermilk   10
For Irving and Stanley   12
Still   14
Referred Pain/Remember Grace   15
Clerestory   17
Snow Day   18
Moonsong I   19
Novercal Lullabye   20
Songline   21
Spring Proof   22
Stray Sod   24
Special Interests   26
Soul Tea   27
To Rise and Shine   30
Witness   32
Art History   33
21st Century   35
Trianon   36
Fanning the Flames   37
Blind Spot   38
Intimacy   39
Kairos   41

Tikkun   43
Night Kitchen   44
Night Blooming Wings   45
Living with Loss and a Lathe   46
Terpsichore   47
Lunch with a Long-Lost Friend   48
Prayer for the Spiders Displaced by My Broom   49
Sapphires   51
Blessing   52
In the Spirit of Water   53
Con Brio   55
Juxtaposition   57
Homo Con Brio   58
Continuum   59
Daddy's Girl   61
Inside Job   63
For Nick, Who Gave Me the Ocean   64
Nameless   65
Dreamflight   66
Light Loving Light 68
Moon Jar Freefall   69
Astroplankton Break Dance   70
Saltwater Slam Dance   71
Noctiluca Sojourn   72
Old Friends   73
An Overdue Reply   75
Two Aspects   77
Cantillation   78
Pilgrimage   79
Escape Velocity   80
Maiden Voyage   81

Halfway Home   83
Salt and Fire and Time   84
Apoptosis   85
Embracing My Shadow   87
Thin Places   88
New Year's Day Feme Sole   89
Moonsong II   91
Gravitation/Levitation   92
Go Slow   93
Shenandoah   95
Aging   96
Countdown to Wholeness   97
Mercy   99
Immolation   100
Leave Taking   101
Mirabile Dictu   102
Hands   103
In the End   105

Spring Planting

When a poem comes for you
It opens you like a plow:

First the seizing, then the cutting,
Then the being tumbled over –

All so the seeds can find the place
Where spirit and elements converge.

Jive Child

I am a rhythm-driven creature
craving meter,
The more elliptical the beat,
the better.

Under Mother's steady heart,
capricious child with fragile wiring grew,
tuned to the key of syncope.

Jive child,
wild as the roadside weeds
on the way to Graceland.

Infusion

Everywhere you touch the ocean
    she lights up;
each wave and fish and footstep
    stirs the fire.
Her bioluminescent tide outshines
    the moon!

I long to inhabit a body
    where ideas shimmer,
each respiration
    in - can - desces,
and poems carom through me
    like slingshot stars.

Far from the ocean,
    I harbor-tend her embers.
In a Shenandoah version
    of aurora borealis
I strike river rocks
    into startled, short-lived sparks.

Drawn by the smoke and mystery,
    pyrotechnic poems
tunnel like ship worms through my bones,
    investing them with light;
teasing open atoms
    to inhale my salt and fire.

Where it Comes From/Deep Within

Covering your back in poetry,
tracing with my finger
the mnemonic figures needed
to preserve my thoughts
'til daybreak illumines pad and pencil.

All the dark hours I continue creating
without waking you,
covering your back with poetry
etched in light,
saving in memory and skin
the warm thoughts of the shared night.

At dawn you stretch and rise
and I reach for the paper
to recreate what even now you are
washing unseen from your skin,
vowels racing down the drain.

Litmus Test

After washing each other's hair
and bundling up in towels
you patiently untangle
the stubborn knot in the
fine chain of the necklace
you brought from Utah
and fastened 'round my neck
on our first date years ago.

If ever our daughter asks
I will tell her:

Everything that matters
lies in moments like these;
this is how you know it's love.

Accommodation

I am the chief cartographer of your contours,
Having weathered over the years into
    a wax casting
Fitting your every angle and rib;
More familiar with your topography
Than even the troughed and feathered bed
We have shared for three decades.
Perfect correspondence.

When you are gone, I recast the missing
Counterpart, settling instead
For your pillows curved against
My mirrored shape of you.
Only when I walk bare skinned
In the rain do I soften, expand,
And reclaim my own shape again.

L'arc-en-ciel

Our hugs: greeting, parting, celebrations.
    Quiet rituals, sacred to me, our hugs
Are peace, passion, humanity shared.

Heaven is not a separate reality when
    Touch and transcendence are one.

Let Emily have her buzzing fly.
    When I die I'll savor the Quintessential.
Our hugs: rites of passage, affirmation.

Heaven is not apart from Earth
when Touch and Transcendence are one.
Help my bones sing hymns to life.
    Hug me. Now!

That Time of Year

Wanting to write a poem
I rinse brown rice,
slice ginger, sprinkle thyme,
roast the aromatic roots,
boil the rice in fragrant stock.

When the windows sweat with steam,
I write a poem in the frost
signed with a melting thumbprint.

In the shadow of starlit verse
hearts of onion curl open and crisp,
hissing their pleasure when
    dropped in the soup:
communion clear and simple.

Still Life with Buttermilk

The buttermilk shimmers with holiness.
Palming the sweating bottle –
its promising heft, the shock of cold –
pouring a tumbler
just more than half full.

Drawing blood, drawing a life,
perspectives converge at the vanishing point.
Foreshortening only makes plain –
What's closest looms largest –
while the future recedes from view.

Routine blood work, stick and run,
never a second thought until
jangling phone, the doctor saying
"Unexplained anomalies…
extremely large cells…"

Online expedition
in search of the well-guarded truth.
Destiny hides from the casual seeker.
Knowledge appropriates fear.
Quitting is out of the question.

At 4 AM the keywords

macrocystosis+monocytosis+
    secondary+cancer
finally crack the code.
Mother lode of detail
worth the sleep lost searching.

Some truths hold, regardless of scale.
In the soul of the world –
or the night of one soul – whoever said,
"The past is prologue" got it right.
Poets trade in tempests,
recounting the siege of humors fair and foul.

Revelation strips presumption
    down to its homespun socks.

Here is everything I know:

Life begins with this glass of milk,
perishable benediction
against the coming dawn.

For Irving and Stanley,
Your Dad and Mine

You try to digest all his words and their
    meaning:
One line still echoes, "It's cancer...*cancer.*"
You get home, start your tractor and
    head for the field
to plow and think, to work and to wait
for the earth always answers your needs.

There were times when you didn't have two
    cents between you
but you managed somehow to survive
    and pull through
the odd jobs, the lean years, the hot
    sun and tough weeds
you prayed and you planted your
    crops and your dreams
believing the earth always answers
    your needs.

The children, like angels tap dancing in puddles
with puppies and parasols, high heels and boots
brought wonder and laughter and tadpoles
    and tears.
You tended your garden of kids and tomatoes

knowing the earth always answers your needs.

Gently return to the earth that has raised you.
Harvest your dreams and sit down for a rest.
The land that is home will one day enfold you
and welcome you back to its peaceful breast.
Travel in grace, for you've always believed
the earth will forever answer your needs.

Still
(for Ray)

A pot of boiling water
becomes a simple hearth
in times of need or want.

Curving your body into the simmer
to steam up your face or ease your chill
or summon the friend
whose campfire
drew your circle together
until his heart gave out…

He would have liked this scene –
nothing more than what is needed:
a practical moment of comfort and grace,
this found poem being lived,
his memory distilling from vapor.

Referred Pain/Remembered Grace

When you go faint from inflicted grief
You suddenly notice how many
Hard surfaces the world contains:
Slate, hearthstones, table saw,
Heart baked to granite by rage…
And this is just the short list.

On the way down you remember to peek
Beneath your assumptions, newly aware
That even the most obdurate are spacious
Constellations of light-emitting energy
Dancing in their chosen masquerades.

Does not make the landing any softer
Knowing this. Does not call back
Into wholeness the exploded shards
Of your soul, or explain why love
Unloaded its gun into you.

It <u>does</u> invite you to smile as you hit the floor.

From here it is all a ride home.
Worm food or spirit flight – whichever
Vehicle of transcendence you take –

You arrive at the very same dance:
The knees that used to ache with grief
Shatter now into songs of light.

Clerestory

Against five contrails roughly parallel
And rich in the late fall light
Comes a ragged line of geese.

Looking up, she scans the score
Then journeys on, humming
Celestial riffs, unburdening a heart
More birdsong than blues.

Snow Day

We are in snow
and well:
Like crocus bulbs
fat with stillness,
risking peace
before the demands
of growth.

Moonsong I

Though we live in the city
We are farmers in our way;
Each month we seek fertile ground.

We plant by the moon:
I drop a seed
You plow the furrow.

Just as for a harvest of corn
The wooden crib is waiting.

Novercal Lullaby

She shrinks the footprint
Of her love
To fit the plot they ceded.
Barely a toehold,
But knowing the strength
Of roots,
She entrusts her seed
To the earth
And dreams her bonsai
Into being.

Songline

When you come to a place
where the roots are so old
they smell like roasted bones,

perception ... pivots.

There are homing beacons
stronger than hurricanes–
or reason.

Rain remembers everything.
One drink from this spring
will confirm all your dreams.

Spring Proof

Spring proof at the dam:
On my knees in the pipe I peer for eels
as thin and long as pins.
Water arcs 'round my boots;
despite wool socks, my toes go blue.

Eels you can see through!
Back home I plop one in a well slide
filled with brackish water
and focus the microscope lens.
The elver's deep red heart beats so fast
I can't keep up the count.

What must it make of the light?
How far must it feel from home?
Yet when the time is right
(a dozen years from now)
it will leave this fresh pond
to seek a salt tide,
head back to the ocean
and spawn.

Is that taught by smell and sight?
Born in the egg and sperm?
Or is it faith?

Its dot of a brain holds a map
of more of the world than I shall ever see.

Dropping the elver back in the jar
I row once more to the dam.
On my knees, I tip the glass
and give life back to life.

Stray Sod

In the grocery store you are at first quiescent –
A relief after the fuss you put up,
<u>Insisting</u> on wearing your clothes inside-out,
Citing Celtic tradition.

When we reach the oranges, you are overcome.
Your internal dial spins again
And you grab and grope, pulling my blouse,
Nuzzling me with your whiskery chin.

I want to scream, "I don't kiss strangers!"
But catch myself in time. It is unfair;
You have no awareness of person or place.
Blame has no role here.

Someone runs for the manager. Meanwhile,
I disentangle from your grasp, re-button
My blouse, remember to breathe.
You recede like a tide into stillness.

When the out-of-breath manager asks,
"Ma'am, are you all right?"
I tear up, about to explain your condition.
Before I can speak, you clear your throat.

Unruffled, you brush imagined indignities
From your sleeve, declaring, "Everything's fine
Now. My wife... she has these episodes,
But everything's back to normal now."

Smiling through prisms of tears, I see you:
As gallant and kind in this savage decline as
Anyone could be. Clasping hands, we go forth
To claim the odd fortunes this day still contains.

Special Interests

I am struck by the easy way
you reach for my parcels,
and move to block the chilly wind.
You compliment my shoes.

I have loved you long enough to know
this is both apology and bridge building.
You trust in me to recognize this is touching.
We have loved for so long we can fill in the
　gaps.

On the sidewalk in front of the Capitol
I forgive you almost by instinct.
In accord once more, we turn and go in,
a fearless united front.

Soul Tea

At tea with my soul the other day
        I was astonished to learn

That peace is the product
        of careful propagation.

The living seed must find rich ground
        in order to grow in the heart

Old feelings can be recycled
        into nourishing compost

Creating encouragement
        from pain, laughter, tears and
        disappointment

Nothing is ever lost, only reconfigured

All that was once hurtful or happy can recombine
        to nourish the seedling of peace

Emotional compost renews the soul,
        clearing the attic to feed the roots

Preparing the soil is thoughtful work…

Like making a Zen rock garden,

    Or tending to your dreams,

        Or cultivating passion.

Recycled sun provides the warmth, but peacelings must be watered.

Living waters

    Of compassion,

        Awareness,

           Humility,

                And oneness

Give the rootlets what they need

    To strengthen their grip and

        Support new growth

           As they reach to the stars

with confidence, trepidation

and hope.

Without the roots beneath the soil

We'd never learn to soar.

To Rise and to Shine

Up 'til now I've been plowing the lower forty,
faithfully tilling the soil for whatever came next.

Today, at forty, I straighten to face the middle
    ground,
looking ahead to the harvest, when –
strengthened by the sun and rain –
I'll rise like a heavy-headed stalk of grain
pushing upwards to the source.

The view from the field, with its deepening
    furrows, is painted in ripening desert tones.
Amber, rose, sage and smoke color
    my taproot dreams.
The shadows lengthen.
The winds begin to carve the shape
    of the life that I have lived.
They blow somber, joyful notes, playing my
    hollowing bones like flutes.

And still I rise like leavened bread baked by
 experienced hands.
And rising, shine my light on something fresher
 than convention
to illumine interior landscapes of magic.

Witness

Watching your stalwart heart
freighted to gray with depression,
I am helpless to defend in any way.
Unable to fathom your journey,
wanting to lend support,
I offer my bony shoulder
to your task, and am felled
at once to my knees.

The weight of your pain would
drop a Clydesdale in her prime.
But when I reframe the dynamic,
trusting the earth to hold the weight,
I pull the rest like a plow,
breaking new ground as I go.

Hoping to ease your way, prayers –
like seeds – fall into each furrow.
Planting by the moon,
I envision your harvest of light.

Art/History

I recall declaring archly to a friend
that in marriage <u>I</u> had not ceded
the rights to <u>my</u>self.
I pitied his domestication,
his voluntary loss of freedom
to associate with whom he chose –
and when.

But life splinters our convictions,
challenging the intentions
we declared with such passion
on another, more theoretical day.

Staring out from your supremely
self-contained self-portrait,
you give new vision:
how brute self-reliance looks
to one whose own edges, ragged,
seek counterpoint in close relation.

The lesson is stark, for it is you I love
and long for, you with your own self,
unavailable to me;
smooth as polished pecan shells.

My years-ago friend had his wife
in trade for his freedom.
I stand free but empty-handed,
trumped by your retained first option,
your sole sovereignty over yourself.

A different means to a familiar end:
completing the loop to find you
standing in my old shoes.

Wisdom derives from nuance:
recoil of recognition,
the shadings of longing,
that love-is-an-unlisted-number look
veiling the eyes
staring down
from your portrait.

21st Century

I am the victim of a religious education
That made me fear freedom more than the veil.
I prize my faith as much as any man.
Why must I hide to prove it?

I might wear the veil proudly, if I could choose.
But decreed, it is no honor.
The tyrants brag, feeling smug
That their women are well in hand.

It is hard to take pride in shame.

Trianon

Let others practice social grace
And hone their deadly wiles;
I cultivate indifference,
Ignore at point-blank range.

Loving care can be unlearned,
Heartstrings reeled back in.
Like a lungfish in a drought:
Retreat, conserve and wait for rain.

Terminally poised, cool as a corpse,
I saw you at last night's reception.
With my back to you both, I adopted
A stranger, and talked an erudite game.

I heard you laugh and passed so close
That I dusted your knees
With my wayward skirt.
My heart lay still, no spark at all
As triumph extinguished old flames.

Fanning the Flames

October eventide, fresh-scrubbed and glowing
Golden leaves and green
Glint against rain-blackened bark
Beauty in extremis.

We pitch our tent under the gingko tree
And commence the wait for Magic
Sitting vigil for the golden deluge
Full splendor of loving
Under bushels of tiny golden fans
All letting go together.

Blind Spot

She wears shrouds of unborn wings: silk
jacket fluttering against her burnished skin.
Pacific bivalves were wrenched apart to
plunder the pearls that encircle her throat.

Planting her feet, rooted to her mother orb,
she opens her mouth and convicts every heart
within hearing: "Peace is a daily decision.
You each have the power to heal this planet.
Make every choice with love!"

Within the crowd, the assassin slowly
inhales -- the reverse of a ragged sigh –
and brings the blowgun to his lips.

Intimacy

You opined that I might shun intimacy. Perhaps you are right, but this I know:

I have sat quietly with the dying;
   knelt close to those who strained
      to coordinate muscles to form their words.

Showered with saliva, I have blinked
   to clear my eyes but never flinched,
     straining almost as hard
        to listen as the speakers fought to speak.

I have discussed sex aids in public places
   when someone needed candid answers
and placed a urinal around the penis
   of a man too weak from AIDS
     to manage such a simple necessity.
And I did it without rubber gloves.

Fear of intimacy? Maybe.

Still, when my times of need arrive,
   I hope there will be someone present:
To wait 'til I can get my thoughts out,
To do what I cannot do for myself,

To value each second of our shared
    and amazing life,
To gaze upon my suffering without
    looking away,
To hold my hand during scary procedures,
To stand up and fight when I cannot
    rally on my own behalf,
To tell the truth when it is hard,
And through whatever comes,
    To love the me inside the struggle.

Intimacy has so many definitions! I don't know how else to reply.

Kairos

*Wonderful to do when the power goes out,
and your home is candle-light silent.*

Touch a match to candlewick,
Quarter a fragrant orange.
Pry the flesh from the rind,
Inhaling its refreshment.

Separate the sections into a bowl
Where they can rest and respire.
Distill your peace to its luminous core
Then invoke a panoply of awe.

Take up a shard of orange rind;
Hold it near the candle fire.
Fold over the tip, pith against pith
And finger-press.

Blessing the flame with oil
Keep working the rind at intervals,
Releasing fireworks and essence
In each of the Four Directions.

Do this in remembrance,
To give thanks, or heal the world.

Using everyday ingredients,
Quicken the air with zest.

Return to the sections of fruit in the bowl,
Bite through the taut skin into liquid light
Ululating grace as you imbibe
With all of your senses.

Inhale the scene into all of your bones
And blow out the candle flame in peace.
Lie down to rejoin the world of dreams
Knowing the smoke will complete the prayer.

Tikkun

Red beans, vanilla and tamarind,
the steep silence of this inner room:
Soapstone flecked with mica dust,
dozens of handmade paper doves
sparkle-drying on the rack.

The blades of her shoulders unfold into flight
as the kettle whirrs to a whistle.
The beeswax balance of spirit and matter
Glazes her life like Winesap and honey.
Forgiveness complete, the new year begins.

Night Kitchen

The blue irises of the gas burners
stare at the ceiling all night long,
dreaming of the stars.

Late-Blooming Wings

The stream so busy washing light
against the obdurate rocks
reminds your weary heart:
it is possible to be beat half to death
and still rise up to shine.

You with your late-blooming
wings
are come to the table at last.

Fractures refract the light;
nothing is where it appears to be.
Blood is thicker than water;
spirit, lighter than air.

Living with Loss and a Lathe

You valued a piece of old chestnut post,
because it grows no more.

Turned it gently on your lathe
into a graceful vessel,

proud that the gaping holes did not
prevent its creation,
happy they are part of the finished piece:
cherished as one of a kind.

Terpsichore

What a force field! Or maybe just
the potential to evoke response.

Deliberate friction of palm against
palm, rustling dry sparks,
recalling the gesture you made before
words: warming your palms and
traversing your arms then
slowly speaking your truth.

And your final dance!
Controlled eruption inciting each
mutant cloistered spark.
Voracious Gladiator!
Despite the years, I still
burn my hands
on the memory of you.

Lunch with a Long-Lost Friend

Clean, strong October winds
still stir the leaves of my heart.
They fall open to a long-ago page,
and time spirals backwards,
like a perfect touchdown pass.

Prayer for the Spiders Displaced by My Broom

(Remember that spider is the keeper of knowledge of the primordial alphabet. – Ted Andrews, <u>Animal Speak</u>)

Print shops get dusty; the slide-worn type cases,
all the two-legged to-ing and fro-ing
    setting the lines,
proofing and printing, binding the pages,
    distributing type;
all with the doors rolled wide to wind
    and bamboo leaves.

This treasury of minute pieces incites
    recombination,
creative mutation and hesitant ruin;
    these words and images
pressed into paper the webs we leave
    in our wake.

Three steps in the door I skid on the dusty floor,
revising the afternoon plans.
    Ignoring the vacuum,
I reach for the broom, preserving the quiet
so full of promised words that this room holds
    like a temple.

Sweeping by sections, approaching with care,
 giving the newly home-wrecked spiders
time to scramble before herding dirt into
 dustpan.
Repetition, presence, silence, sweat: all as lovely
 as hours spent setting a poem.

But the spiders!

Anyone who has ever lost their grip,
 dropping a tray's weight
of tiny lead type knows something of
 the chore ahead for each
of these eight-legged refugees:
re-creating ordered beauty
despite the odds that the broom will
 come again.

Pausing like Kali in the door I give
 them John McCutcheon's
words, "I bow my life and offer
 grace," then leave the spiders

to merge into evening wafture, so full
 of loss and tribute.

Sapphires

After one of the sapphires
went on a walk about, its
empty bezel a dry socket
beside the winking blue eye
of its twin: One stone of truth
loose in the world; one still in
her wedding band, she ponders
the implications.

Blessing

New wears away faster
than you can polish the silverplate
off the wedding candlesticks.
You have to plan ahead.

In the beginning you seek one another
as frankly as magnets.
The trick is to learn to court forever,
like fireflies
refusing to lose that flame.

As darkness falls, their sparks
count even more, a rhythmic blessing
foretelling the hearth fires of winter
where first two, then one, then no one
sits to tend the embers.

But sparks fly up the chimney.
So too with your souls,
leaving gravity behind,
expanding the meaning of love,
giving the fireflies
something to shoot for.

In the Spirit of Water

for Malidoma

Stirring the shells as fluid as granulated water
I swirl them until the esteemed elder says,
"Good." He studies their configuration
on the colorful divination cloth
spread out between us.

A few minutes later
this luminous man imparts,
"Here, you look like a tree --
the trees see you as one of them!"

His words continue in splashes and torrents,
a river of confirmation and the sweet contiguity
among all things. Fresh eucalyptus
infuses the air
with music that makes revelation feel at home.

In the end, I bow and hand him a story,
an offering.

With a twinkle, I wonder whether he has
already divined its contents

or will he laugh to read:
"Seen through the eyes of a leaf,
what color is the sky?"

Con Brio

Sybaritic summer fridge overstuffed
with sugar peas, cherries, blueberries
and eggplant bulbous as a dream
bubble full to bursting –
as we are, in the twilight,
roasting marshmallows over waning coals,
watching fireflies in the dusk,
telling lies and laughing.

From your corner no sound,
but purest motion as – eyes closed –
you conduct Mahler's 9th
with zucchini stick baton.
Tempura batter clings faithfully
to the vegetable instrument through
andante and allegro.
You conduct the work with love,
unabashed to be seen
leading an invisible orchestra
with a squash shard.

Moonlight polishes your bald skull
and hollows the cavities of your eyes
in shadow. The skin on the bridge
of your nose gleams platinum,

alchemy of sweat plus sunlight
bounced off the moon and sent again
to the earth, planet twice kissed
by its sun.

The dogs sniff our plates, lingering
over melted cheese and fettucine
petrified to translucence
in the cool evening air.

At such moments, forever seems
too small a space to fill.

Juxtaposition

She is wormy chestnut;
you, quarter-sawn tiger maple
chatoyant in the sun.

Her antique cells thrum cicada song,
kindred soul of cycles.
She is the blood red moon.

Your self-sufficient brilliance sings out loud
against her holy, hand-waxed planks.

On certain summer nights,
the cedar eaves' hot respiration
mingles with lavender's longing.

Heat lightning quickens
your flame, and the crickets
grow giddy with love.

Homo Con Brio

We root at the breast of wonder
all our lives, seeking
the next great feast.

We strike our match selves
against rough stone, longing
to bloom into light.

We arrive, primed and primal.
All other pursuits
are foreplay or fuel.

Continuum

for Susan and Mattison

You are born with every egg intact and
at attention. Each moonstone you wear,
every sandy soil tomato you ingest,
each aria and scale you set free
infuses the juice that feeds them,
sending messages light years ahead.

Decades from now when your daughter asks,
"Remember the white house with the violet
door and the butterfly bush out front?"
you will marvel. You last saw that place
when you were six. There are not photographs;
you have not spoken of it since childhood.

But the memories live as deep in your heart
as her egg was tucked in your ovary, twin
cotyledons on the space-time continuum.
She must have heard them singing all along!
Germination has many tunnels and triggers
and infinite frontiers.

A lifetime from now when a future grand-
daughter – the one who carries a peacock

plume everywhere she goes, the one with the soul of an amethyst – asks her mother, "Remember the snail with the orange shell and brilliant turquoise eyes?" her eggs will sparkle and sing, inciting their own magic dreams.

Daddy's Girl

We each want the other's pain,
when we are not the source.
It is easier to shoulder the load
than to watch a dear one struggle.
When I had cancer it was your prayer
that you could take my place.
Now our roles are reversed,
and with them the wish:
Let me take this for you.

This is a lovingly leveraged buy-out,
the calling in of a note.
An eye for an eye, a heart for a heart,
I'll cover your offer and raise the bid.
Take my love, our laughter, my thanks —
but you may not have my disease.
I don't want to be well at your expense; tell
God the deal has changed.

This dance we do will end in tears.
One of us has to go first.
But maybe where there's love enough,
there's health to go around.
So you keep well, live long in joy,
and lead by robust example.

I'll follow in your wake,
if I cannot match your stride,
and be blessed by each day that we share.

Inside Job

Under the shelter of my tented knees,
you beam like a campfire,
then flicker in and out of starlit sleep.

Your cancer hit so hard
there was no time for your
Make-a-Wish trip to the redwoods.

We ordered sequoia wallpaper, glued it
to a sturdy bolt of canvas, and curled it
about your hospital bed like a diorama.

Not even Lewis & Clark beheld constellations
like the glow-in-the-dark shapes pasted
onto the ceiling above.

Cocooned in your homemade sleeping bag
with openings for your IVs, G-tube and other
strands of life support, you look translucent:
a pupa at rest; your cells coalescing into wings.

After a lifetime of munching in the forest of
your dreams, you wait only for a freshet of wind
to seek your next frontier.

For Nick, Who Gave Me the Ocean

In violet depths an oyster sits secreting,
womb to a nacreous secret.
Somewhere the cacophony begins,
timpani waves come crashing in.
Haunting is the seaflute blowhole's chant.
In tropical champagne brine, crown jewels glide
(and sharks).

While in the bay the moon's silver inlays
throb and pulse,
aching in my throat, reflecting in salty tears,
the depths stir, begin to broil
and lash, the tears well up
and shimmer.

And I wonder which side of my eyelids
the tempest is really on.
The seaflute blowhole answers
"Ommmmmmm"
while the oyster takes a nap.

Nameless

Dancing on the edge of consciousness,
teasing my tongue with the taste of its vowels,
I still cannot call your name.

I remember its sibilance,
know that it suits you,
recall it reminds me of seaweed and rice.
Still, I cannot call your name.

The details of our acquaintance are fully intact
and at my fond disposal.
All that I lack is the name on the file drawer
   handle.

Nameless, but with a warmth that
   overtakes me,
I reach for your hand,
secure that our history
will carry the day,
redeeming even senility.

Dreamflight

In naps where my brain knits itself back
    together
I find letters from lovers long dead.
'Ere I can unfold them my dreams change
    channels
Leaving the letters unread.

Channel surfing in my dreams
Lets me browse wide but not deep.
Channel surfing in my dreams
I travel so far in my sleep!

In slumbers each night where I go to
    recharge,
Scenes from the future unwind.
They leave me to wake just to ponder
    what's real
And to search for the meaning of time.

In daydreams I catnap to find scraps of peace
Amid hectic happenings, wild disarray.
The seconds of sweetness my visions renew
Before I'm snapped back to the fray.

Channel surfing in my dreams

Gives me a moment's surcease.
Channel surfing in my dreams
High flight on my mental trapeze.

Channel surfing in my dreams
Where no boundaries exist between tenses.
Channel surfing in my dreams
To explore the full range of the senses.

Channel surfing in my dreams
Lets me browse wide but not deep.
Channel surfing in my dreams
I travel so far in my sleep!

Light Loving Life

In this small town
You are competition for the oxygen
In short supply.

We shrink to round sparks of spirit-blue
When what we long for is to stretch
Our own full height toward the sun,
Peaking, pointing, pirouetting;
A gambol of light,
Combustion at its simple best.

We were born to stretch, but also to flicker.
In my dreams I am a comet's tail
Streaking through the night.

Moon Jar Freefall

A shiver of moonlight
slips between clouds
to finger a jar on your sill,
sending it arcing
toward the receptive slate.

Whole at last
the shards explode,
setting the fireflies free.

Astroplankton Break Dance

Leads you to a place:
Where hope is embraced
Where escape becomes reality
Where the universe is redefined
Where possibilities are probabilities
Where language eludes expression
Where boundaries are detonated
Where perspective is enhanced
& the soul is uplifted

Saltwater Slam Dance
(once upon a time in Florida)

Snorkeling off an Atlantic beach we must
traverse fire coral to reach the open water.
Our only opportunity lies in the cresting wave.

If our timing is off, we'll be set down
belly first on the sharp and stinging coral
until the next wave's grace.

Like city kids on a sidewalk leaping into
twirling ropes to do a double-dutch dance,
we rock in rhythm to several passing waves.

Once our bodies are calibrated, we each hail a
wave, then desperately flail to clear the coral
in the two seconds of lift.

This is the point of being alive.
Nowhere but the ocean plays this hard,
and for such tender, high-flown stakes.

Noctiluca Sojourn

Everywhere you touch the ocean
she lights up; each wave and
fish and footstep stirs the fire.
Her bioluminescent tide outshines
the moon!

I long to inhabit a body
where ideas shimmer,
each respiration incandesces,
and poems carom through me
like slingshot stars.

Old Friends

Counting the seconds between lightning and
 thunder,
You pronounce the water safe.
I freeze in the late night pool
But would rather turn blue than stop talking.
We are old friends.

When you see me shiver, you come out too,
And give me the biggest towel you own.
We are old friends.

When I ask a pointed question, you
 reply with a look
That would wither anyone else.
 It does not deter my persistence.
We are old friends.

I can double as your cousin, your ex-wife,
 your sister.
We are old friends.

I know better than to laugh with you
 at how she fields a softball.
I hear the fondness in your voice –
 and can tell you love the girl.

We are old friends.

When I try to cajole you into dancing,
   you pull a Seal Team Maneuver,
showing me how you could break my arm
   and crack my skull.
We must appear strange to strangers!
We are old friends.

Even your girlfriend doesn't worry.
She knows that I know what's important to you.
We are, after all, old friends.

An Overdue Reply

At six I lacked the words to say that
faced with competing demands – the can of
fiddler crabs suddenly spilled in the sink,
the prospect of missing the school bus home –
I did the best I could.

Leaving the crabs scrabbling against porcelain,
each clacking its oversized claw and
   auburn shell
and even its tiny claw against the others,
I ran for the impatient bus.

Next morning, breathless,
I entered the classroom I loved,
spatula in hand, ready to round the fiddlers
back up, only to start at your wrath,
and at the stark, silent sink.

How could I have known it would frighten you
(You: So grown up! So capable!)

to discover that sink full of angry claws
after a long day of loving away all our first
   grade fears?
Overwhelmed, so unnerved you killed them all.

Stunned, having never even seen you cross;
winnowed by guilt, over all the wild lives lost
I trembled, full of feelings so beyond the reach
of words. I'd meant only to take the fiddlers
to show and tell their salt marsh beauty,
then carry them back to their birthright.

Forty years later I run my fingers
    through this bowl
of empty pistachio shells, their salty,
crystalline sound a lullaby of atonement,
an elegiac throwing of the bones
for lives I meant to borrow but a day.

A sound not unlike a death rattle, or the
crushing of exoskeletons against porcelain,
or the eggshell of innocence hitting the floor;
the sting of air on salty flesh the price
of understanding.

Two Aspects

Spent-winged, triumphal,
The morning sprite stirs.
Willow-trim and weightless
From a night of journeyed dreaming,
Her eyes still reflect other worlds.

By bedtime she has ripened.
Buddha-bellied and comely,
Well provisioned for the quest,
She is gravid with wonder:
About to be born.

Cantillation

Coming home to my life after years in exile,
I cross the verdigris threshold
back into sacred space.

Poetry is a form of conjuring
the holy water of home,
feeding our roots as nothing else can.

The necessary season of drought has passed,
its hard tack lessons learned by heart.
At last the moisture returns.

Fierce roots – protective, dormant – revive
with fresh advent of rain. Diamond water
sparks the tender green seeking of light.

May I receive equal wisdom in joy
as I was given in exile. May this journey
keep breaking me open.

Pilgrimage

Stumbling down the hall, eyes closed,
The walk of the dead, shuffling gently along.
I lift the lid and let go a stream of
   musical waters
Dancing a sound as clear as the
   laughter of stars.

I yawn and thank St. Exupéry for the image
then pad back to the warmth of flannel sheets.
Pulling my dreams up around my ears
I return to the land of the living.

Escape Velocity

As a girl, all long bones and angles,
she could barely stay upright no matter
how tightly she laced her skates.
Lifelong, she has marveled at those
who dance the ice on razor's edge,
spirits so balanced, their bodies can fly.

The older she grows, the more fiercely
she studies their moves, certain that
if she can flip the equation, equilibrate
her failing body with the precision of love,
her spirit wings will shake loose
to spiral, sun-limned, on the thermals.

Radiant, she fingers her grandfather's
eagle bone flute, calibrating the
sweet sequence of notes to initiate
her personal launch code,
calling every part of herself
laughingly, dancing, home to the fire.

Maiden Voyage

Her heart needs a firewall
or failing that, a fallout shelter
built to withstand the wildcat rages
that detonate domestic ease
into heat-seeking blades of shrapnel.

In quest for armor, she commissions the
blacksmith, "Forge a storm home for my heart,
a place I can fill with unguents and music.
Fit the hinges true, and
hammer a wind-worthy hasp.

"Fire this temple again in the coals
then burnish the edge
with a fine brass brush,
that all the world may see:
Herein beats a gold star heart."

Bereft of safe harbor,
she rises yet
in the lightness of armor
to set her sails
and fly.

Half-Way House

God must have a half-way house
For those not fit for heaven,
To give them time to grow their wings
And finish preparations.

Giving up the earth is hard,
When earth is all you've known.
There must be stairs for each to climb
According to each need.

Some are fit to fly right in
While others need to amble
To linger in transition
Move at their own speed.

God is love and love finds ways
To open every door.
With time and care we all can rise
To find our home on high.

So God must have a half-way house
For those still on their way
To give them time to grow their wings
And time to learn to fly.

Salt and Fire and Time

Crinkled, dewlapped labia, thin as the
    briny book gills
of a stranded horseshoe crab.
    Gunpowder and sage
– her signature scents – whisper from them still,
whenever she dreams of the sea.

Before she knew that hair could burn,
she fashioned candelabra from aluminum foil,
attaching them to her breasts with tape –
an after dinner candlelight surprise.
(And oh! the *awe* in her birthday lover's eyes!)

Nine years later, sliding into a booth at lunch,
errant strands of Celtic frizz wafted
    across a tea light.
First the ROAR; then the waiter
    slapping at her head!
Smelling like a camp fire she returned
    to her office
amazed at what a candle can incite.

Even now, in her eighties, *every* time
    she hears
the birthday song, or inhales a fragrant curry,

her nipples gather themselves into
 cockles of flame,
and the ocean ruffles her gills.

Apoptosis

Unable to break into dream,
summoned by the new moon's capers,
the wingless human wanders
down the oyster shell lane.

Radiant in the dark,
she reconnoiters by feel.
Pine needles cushion her soles
as she turns into the forest.
Pores flung wide, the night winds
breathe right through her.

Drawn to a barely liminal glimmer,
she studies it at length.
It neither moves nor falters.
Striking a match she kneels
to discover a fish half a mile from the
pond, atop a bed of moss.

She imagines the pumpkinseed's
littoral realm foreclosed
by a crosswise beak; suddenly airborne,
gills slashed by drought,
agape at the unfocused view.

Alit on a branch, the roosting heron
had tossed his catch to better
angle it down his gullet.
With a sudden twitch, the harrowed
swimmer arced to ground, slowly
drying to stillness.

The fish, transcendent in decay,
is a cooling ember deconstructing
into phosphorescence:

Illuminating manuscript
    chiaroscuro still life,
        transubstantiation.

      Microbial midwives decant its light,
  leaving the rest to settle back down

and dream the heron into being.

Embracing my Shadow

Up from the dark the gifts of origin,
shrouded too long in disrepute,
their treasure undimmed by devaluation,
consent to be hauled up in pots
for the blessing of our tables.

Up from the dark the pots long missed,
without which we have hobbled and hurt.
Reintegration – like re-entry – can be risky,
but the vision of wholeness beckons.

Up from the dark our black opal selves,
undifferentiated and connected –
complex blessing of common roots –
give strength to send our own tender green
towards the light, roots deep in home
as we stretch to the source,
finding ourselves in the journey.

Thin Places
(for Robbi)

Impress this day on us the way a
    letterpress printer
set just so bites and debosses the paper,
    reshaping it
for as long as fiber memory holds.

Tattoo our souls with pigment:
    barred owl buff
and brown, your blaze orange parka, our eyes
espresso and aquamarine atop your mountain
amongst ancestors seen and unseen.

Friends smiling as only mortals on high ledges
    do:
straight into wind and leukemia: Clear, clean,
Anchored by this ancient mountain dreaming.

Laughing in the cold coming at us like a train.

New Year's Day Feme Sole

One year we left the tree up
'til Valentine's Day:
Our Southerner's penchant for lingering.

This year: two trees, hold the hearts,
new order for a new decade.
Some breaks are past repair.
Good horses have been put down
over hairline fractures.
It all depends on the injury.

Back in somber fall we adopted Jewish custom,
asking pardon for the past year's blunders.
Grace grants easements for interfaith
borrowing, for anything that heals.

Your card on my mantle put it best:
"Thank you for loving and forgiving me.
I love and forgive you."

Peace was hard to come by during our final
reckoning but now, in this season of miracles
    and light,
of celebrating the harvest home,
we have finally done all right for ourselves.

Southern goodbyes take forever,
but they give love its due.

Moonsong II

Given the present circumstances
The future is a spinster.
Webs never woven leave empty space
(empty womb, empty face).

Months come and go, the ebb and
Flow of opportunities missed.

The thread of generations is a fragile
Line, once broken, forever gone.
I weave meaning from the dailyness
   of life:
Sunflowers, friends, the ocean.

Given the present circumstances
The future is a spinster.
Webs never woven leave empty space
(empty womb, empty face).

By the light of an aging moon
I spin my lament.

Gravitation/Levitation

Gravity has its uses:

The way a tender flank slackens,
nesting like a tea cozy
warming the spent and dreaming secrets
of the lover spooned against its kindred curves.

Under gravity's constant tutelage
connective tissue drops pretense,
unskeins dramatic tension
so the body can expand. . .beyond confines.

The emerging détente between spirit and
  matter
signifies a promise:
In the end, gravity holds the body like a coat,
as spirit skins out and unfurls.

Go Slow

Know the strength of man, but keep a woman's care.
— Lao Tsu

I move slowly.
Sifting and wading through feelings and echoes
that you shuck off like blankets at the sound
of our morning alarm.

I move slowly,
with the power and grace of mindfulness,
of seeing-below-the-surface. You do that
when you paint.   I cannot turn it off.   Ever.

I move slowly,
and bend my schedule to accommodate.
Though I may appear inert, I am
    plying deep waters,
mining meanings in unseen inner caves.

I move slowly,
and with a woman's care,
but remember a saying taught me by a man:
"Go slow and go some mo'."

I smile without hurry
and wonder if my father

even <u>dreamed</u> of all the places
that his phrase would take me.

Shenandoah

She categorically makes her farewells
to each loved one daily –
in meditation,
and again in the middle of the night –
never stopping, even when ill.
Fever itself is a prayer.

Keeping current with each heart
in the constellation frees her
at the end of the world –
for an instant or an eon –
to sit by the Al Hambra,
twirl under Lynn's live oak, and
skinny dip in the Calf Pasture River,
naked before the stars.

One last sensual circuit
of the elemental bases,
a final refinement
before all matter reverts to light:
equally at home in either state.

Aging

I am a woman with whom gravity has
    long since had its way.
Faithless rogue, he wooed in turn my
    body, heart and soul.
Unable to choose, he took each –
    part by part –
until he'd won the drooping whole.

No more tinkling laughter, helium
    orbs, cantilevered parts.
An octave lower,
structural lingerie buoys my spirits
    and orbs.

I used to shoot pictures of dewy
    blossoms at dawn,
flawless petals new and perfect.
Now I like sunflowers late in the day,
    wilted a bit but proud,
resplendent in their disarray,
still turning their faces to the autumn sun,
full of grace and the ripening seeds of
    beauty to come
after winter's dreams.

Countdown to Wholeness

When you see my body, think of raw silk:
its slubs and irregularities are part of its charm.
I live in a vessel whose karma it seems is to play
host to every passing virus and impulse.

The scars and pocks, dimples and dents portray
not lack but loss, and with each loss, new vision.

My cousins have a theory that whatever you
mock in childhood – spider veins, wrinkles –
you later receive in your own life. I would
append: we must <u>do</u> those things that frighten
us, if we are to learn real truths; must risk what
we arrogantly reckon is our own, to learn what
we can do without, and lay claim to the
strength found only in that process.

"Who loses life shall gain it," is open to
interpretations secular <u>and</u> holy.

This long scar is where they took out my spleen,
along with other bits. I am not defined now by
the lack of those assorted parts but by the
knowledge gained after that surgery: how
quickly the body wants to heal! How strong the

cellular instincts to close ranks and get <u>on</u> with it. Acquaintance with the silent power that knits all day and night to mend each break is <u>worth</u> a spleen and more.

With arms, Venus de Milo'd be just another statue. It is who she is <u>now</u> that compels our imagination.

Mercy

Some days the fibers of our being relax,
Leaving room for the spirit winds to
   blow through us.
Touched by new insights we are retuned,
And return to the world with webs of wonder
Woven into warp and woof, marrow and mind.
Some days we are spring cleaned, and
   wake up new.

Some days we are washed by the tearfloods;
Old hurts swept away,
Our walls scrubbed clean of the angry
   graffiti
That clogs their pores with self-doubt.
Some days we are given new nerves
   with which to feel,
Fresh surfaces on which to paint our lives.

Immolation

As floored as I am deeply flawed,
as humbled as razed to cinders,
I will feel with blind hands
For the door which only now is being made.

Wanting to believe, I trust,
as Polly was taught in her dream,
and hope Jesus was true when he said,
"Your faith shall set you free."

If I do not find the door,
I will brood this confinement
'til it hatches a gateway
to larger things than eyes can see.

Leave-Taking

I prefer my demise
    To be no surprise.
I'd rather the hour be of my choosing,
    For I alone know what I'm losing
        And what I stand to gain.

I alone have stood this pain,
Have fought the "noble" fight.
Calling my wits to gather about,
I rage – in my own way –
    'gainst this dying light,
And choose, serenely,
To snuff myself out.

Mirabile Dictu

They always assumed
she was scribbling clinical notations.

After she died they discovered:
She was taking dictation from God.

Poems filled the margins
of her charts,
illuminating empirical data

with larger truths
than numbers can contain.

Hands

Mine are the hands that mucked the stalls
    mine that tended the cows.
Leathery grip once pumped the water,
    scrubbed the troughs and slopped the sows.

The cycles and circles and secrets of all
    only God in his wisdom can know;
Who carries the world in His work-worn palms,
    and its sins on His bloody brow.

Cracked and trembling, gnarled with age,
    sweet chariot please swing low.
Soon let me die; soon let me rot;
    flowers from failing hands may grow.

The cycles and circles and secrets of all
    in fullness can Any One know:
The pungent, the mellow, the dew, the dawn;
    whence did it come and how?

Death is coming, spring's in the air,
    shrouding my barn and my rusting plow.
New wisdom's green vision: blossoming bones,
    burgeoning fern from furrowed brow.

The cycles and circles and secrets of all are
 revealed to each wholeness now.
For I become child become tree become star:
 Thus does a universe grow.

In the End

Let me go like the ginkgo
In a silent shout of glory:

Drop my gold
And lift my arms to heaven.

Made in the USA
Monee, IL
01 September 2021